Bob Chilcott

Mo Li Hua 茉莉花

5 ARRANGEMENTS OF CHINESE SONGS

MUSIC DEPARTMENT

OXFORD
UNIVERSITY PRESS

OXFORD
UNIVERSITY PRESS

Great Clarendon Street, Oxford OX2 6DP,
United Kingdom

Oxford University Press is a department of the University of Oxford.
It furthers the University's objective of excellence in research, scholarship,
and education by publishing worldwide. Oxford is a registered trade mark of
Oxford University Press in the UK and in certain other countries

Database right Oxford University Press (maker)

First published 2015

Impression: 1

ISBN 978-0-19-340421-2

Music and text origination by
Andrew Jones
Printed in Great Britain on acid-free paper by
Halstan & Co. Ltd, Amersham, Bucks.

Contents

Composer's Note

I was asked by David Hill and the Bach Choir to arrange a Chinese folk song for their tour of China in 2014, and I prepared a version of the lovely song 'Mo li Hua'. I loved the melody, which spins its fragile line and, in a Western sense, ends unresolved. With the help of Francesca Mosely, I identified a few more songs from different areas of the country: songs that tell of the beauty of nature, the simplicity of life, and, of course, love. 'Shepherd's Song' was suggested to me by Lin Chun-lung, and I dedicate the remaining four songs in the collection to him and his choir, the Shanghai TMC Mixed Chamber Choir (operated by the Taipei Male Choir). I am grateful both to Francesca and Chun-lung for giving me a glimpse of the diverse and rich culture expressed through each of these songs. They are, of course, arranged from a very Western perspective, but I hope that all types of singers will enjoy the beauty and energy of these traditional melodies. I am also grateful to Sean Bui for his considered editorial work on this publication.

BOB CHILCOTT

作曲家寄语

二〇一四年，大卫•希尔 (David Hill) 及英国巴赫合唱团 (The Bach Choir) 邀请我为其在华演出之旅改编一首中国民歌，我便准备了著名中国民歌《茉莉花》。我非常喜爱《茉莉花》，优美动听的旋律勾勒出花朵娇弱的线条，曲终余音绕梁，让人意犹未尽。在莫鸣 (Francesca Mosely) 的帮助下，我找到了另外几首中国民歌，歌曲诉说自然之美、生活之简、当然，还有爱情之甜。林俊龙向我推荐了内蒙民歌《牧歌》，我也将本曲集后期改编之四首歌献给他及其合唱团——上海拉纤人室内混声合唱团（由台北拉纤人男声合唱团运营）。非常感谢莫鸣和林俊龙，让我透过这些民歌得以一瞥丰富多彩的中华文化。虽然五首民歌以西方人的视角进行改编，但我希望各类型的歌手都能享受这传统旋律传达的美好与活力。最后也要感谢尚恩•裴对本谱集的悉心编辑。

鲍勃•契尔考特

作曲家寄语

二〇一四年，大衛•希爾 (David Hill) 及英國巴赫合唱團 (The Bach Choir) 邀請我為其在華演出之旅改編一首中國民歌，我便準備了著名中國民歌《茉莉花》。我非常喜愛《茉莉花》，優美動聽的旋律勾勒出花朵嬌弱的線條，曲終餘音繞樑，讓人意猶未盡。在莫鳴 (Francesca Mosely) 的幫助下，我找到了另外幾首中國民歌，歌曲訴說自然之美、生活之簡、當然，還有愛情之甜。林俊龍向我推薦了內蒙民歌《牧歌》，我也將本曲集後期改編之四首歌獻給他及其合唱團——上海拉縴人室內混聲合唱團（由台北拉縴人男聲合唱團運營）。非常感謝莫鳴和林俊龍，讓我透過這些民歌得以一瞥豐富多彩的中華文化。雖然五首民歌以西方人的視角進行改編，但我希望各類型的歌手都能享受這傳統旋律傳達的美好與活力。最後也要感謝尚恩•裴對本譜集的悉心編輯。

鮑勃•契爾考特

for Lin Chun-Lung and the Shanghai TMC Mixed Chamber Choir

My Flower
我的花儿/我的花兒

English words by Bob Chilcott

Trad. Chinese
arr. BOB CHILCOTT (b. 1955)

甜,　　　　　哎　　　　　　苗 条 的 姑　　娘 我 把
-lov - - ed,＿＿＿＿＿＿＿＿　All that I wish for　you　is the＿
甜,　　　　　哎　　　　　　苗 條 的 姑　　娘 我 把

酥 油 献 给 你,　　　美 丽 的 姑 娘 我 的 花
fi - nest I＿ can＿ give;　　Beau - ti - ful girl, my flow'r, you bring me＿
酥 油 獻 給 你,　　　美 麗 的 姑 娘 我 的 花

儿, 我要欢 　笑欢 　笑, 哎呀 呀!
joy, you bring me hap-pi-ness;　 ah ya ya ya!
兒, 我要歡 　笑歡 　笑, 哎呀 呀!

4. 虽然我们刚相见, 哎
4. Though we're new-ly met, my be - lov - - ed,____
4. 雖然我們剛相見, 哎

多情的眼睛, 我一见你就倾心,
When I__ see your eyes, my heart is danc - ing with__ the__ flow'rs;
多情的眼睛, 我一見你就傾心,

美丽的姑娘我的花　　儿, 我要欢　　笑欢
Beau - ti - ful girl, my flow'r, you bring me___ joy, you___ bring me___ hap - pi - ness;___
美麗的姑娘我的花　　兒, 我要歡　　笑歡

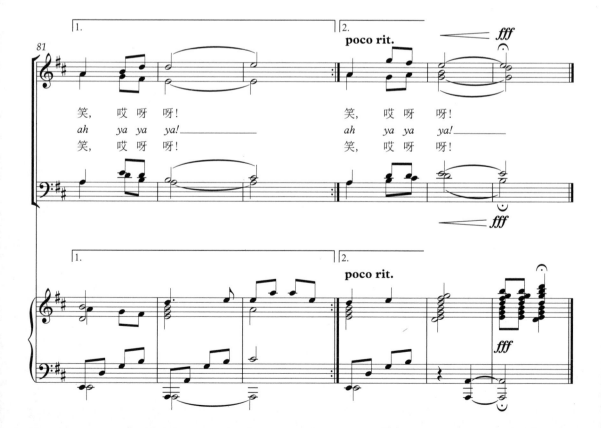

笑, 哎呀呀!　　　　　　笑, 哎呀呀!
ah　ya　ya　ya!___　　　ah　ya　ya　ya!___
笑, 哎呀呀!　　　　　　笑, 哎呀呀!

for Lin Chun-Lung and the Shanghai TMC Mixed Chamber Choir

Shepherd's Song
牧歌

English words by Bob Chilcott

Eastern Mongolian Folksong
arr. BOB CHILCOTT (b. 1955)

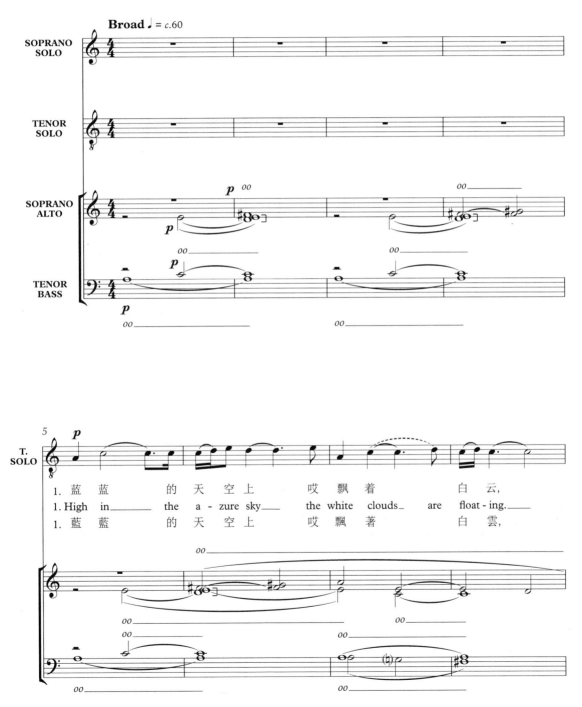

羊群　　　像珍珠　洒在绿绒　　上。
Show - ing___ their beau-ty,___ their_ beau - ty　in___ the_ sun.
羊群　　　像珍珠　灑在綠絨　　上。

*ah*___

*oo*___

rit.

Sun is Out
太阳出来喜洋洋 / 太陽出來喜洋洋

English words by Bob Chilcott

Trad. Chinese
arr. BOB CHILCOTT (b. 1955)

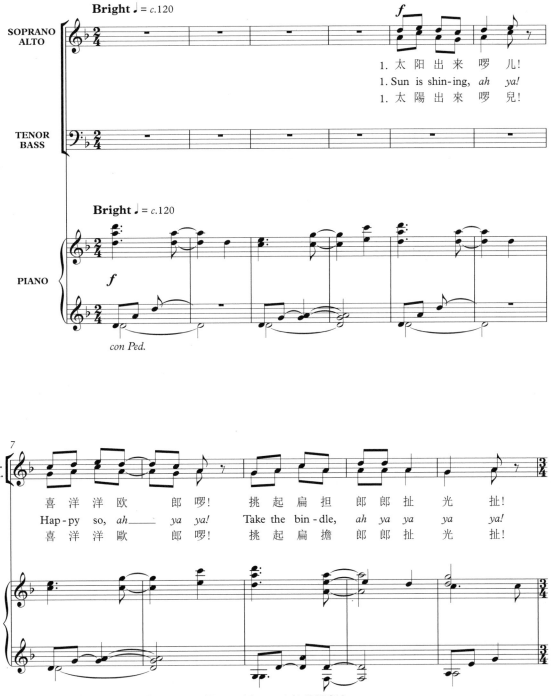

上 山 岗 欧 啰 啰!
Off we go, *ah___ ya ya!_____*
上 山 崗 歐 啰 啰!

T.
B.

2. 手 里 拿 把 啰 儿! 开 山 斧 欧 郎 啰!
2. At the rea - dy, *ah ya!* Axe in hand, *ah___ ya ya!*
2. 手 裏 拿 把 啰 兒! 開 山 斧 歐 郎 啰!

不 怕 虎 豹 郎 郎 扯 光 扯! 和 豺 狼 欧 啰
Ti - gers, jack - als, *ah ya ya ya ya!* We don't care, *ah___ ya*
不 怕 虎 豹 郎 郎 扯 光 扯! 和 豺 狼 歐 啰

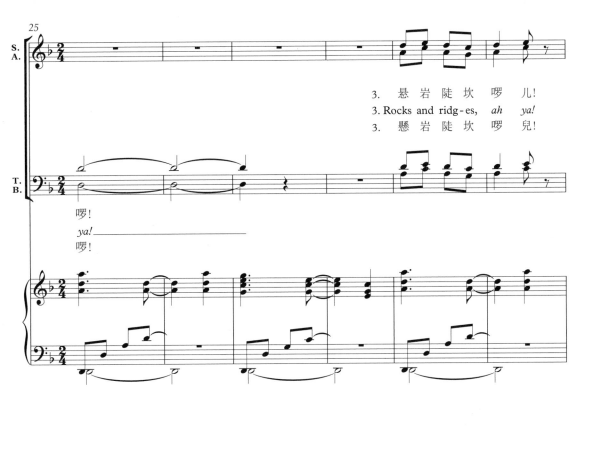

3. 悬 岩 陡 坎 哕 儿!
3. Rocks and ridg - es, *ah   ya!*
3. 懸 岩 陡 坎 哕 兒!

哕!
ya! _____
哕!

不 稀 罕 欧 郎 哕! 唱 起 歌 儿 郎 郎 扯 光 扯!
Show no fear, *ah* _____ *ya ya!* Gath'-ring fire - wood, *ah ya ya ya ya!*
不 稀 罕 歐 郎 哕! 唱 起 歌 兒 郎 郎 扯 光 扯!

36

忙 砍 柴 欧　　 哕　哕!
We　all　sing,　ah_____　ya　　ya!_____
忙 砍 柴 歐　　 哕　哕!

41

4. 走 了 一 山 哕　　 儿!　　又 一 山 欧　　　郎 哕!
4. Cross the moun - tain, ah　　　ya!　　Then one more, ah_____ ya ya!
4. 走 了 一 山 哕　　 兒!　　又 一 山 歐　　　郎 哕!

4. 走 了 一 山 哕　　 儿!　　又 一 山 欧　　　郎 哕!　　这 山 去 了
4. Cross the moun - tain, ah　　　ya!　　Then one more, ah_____ ya ya!　　Then a - no - ther,
4. 走 了 一 山 哕　　 兒!　　又 一 山 歐　　　郎 哕!　　這 山 去 了

这山去了 郎 郎 扯 光 扯！ 那 山 来 欧 啰
Then a - no - ther, *ah ya ya ya ya!* One more gone, *ah ya*
這山去了 郎 郎 扯 光 扯！ 那 山 來 歐 啰

郎 郎 扯 光 扯！ 那 山 来 欧 啰 啰！
ah ya ya ya ya! One more gone, *ah ya ya!*
郎 郎 扯 光 扯！ 那 山 來 歐 啰 啰！

啰！
ya!
啰！

5. 只 要 我 们 啰 儿！
5. Food and cloth - ing, *ah ya!*
5. 祇 要 我 們 啰 兒！

多 勤 快 欧　郎 啰!　　不 愁 吃 来 郎 郎 扯　光　扯!
We don't care, *ah___ ya ya!*　　Work - ing, liv - ing, *ah ya ya ya ya!*
多 勤 快 歐　郎 啰!　　不 愁 吃 來 郎 郎 扯　光　扯!

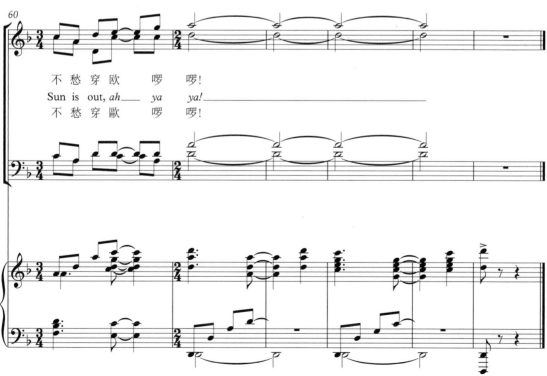

不 愁 穿 欧　啰　啰!
Sun is out, *ah___ ya ya!* _____
不 愁 穿 歐　啰　啰!

for Lin Chun-Lung and the Shanghai TMC Mixed Chamber Choir

In Sichuan
下四川

English words by Bob Chilcott

Trad. Chinese
arr. BOB CHILCOTT (b. 1955)

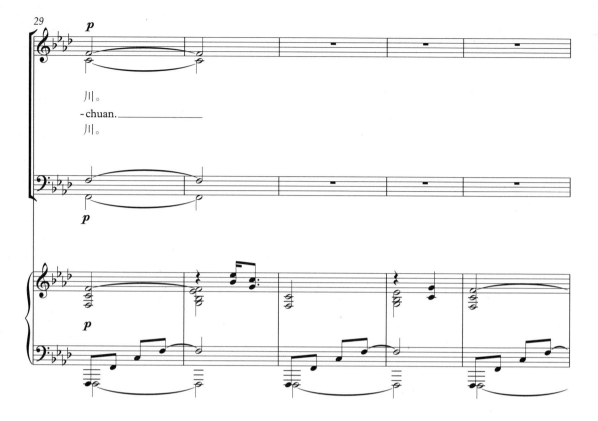

川。
- chuan.
川。

2. 今　个　子　牵　来　者
2. Lead - ing＿ me＿ on - ward,＿
2. 今　個　子　牽　來　者

晚　夕里梦　　见，　噢，　哟
meet＿＿ you＿＿ in＿＿ my＿＿ dreams,　Oh,　oh＿＿
晚　夕裏夢　　見，　噢，　哟

哟，　啊 夜 夜 的 晚　夕里梦
oh,　in the hope I＿＿ meet＿＿ you＿＿ in＿＿＿ my＿＿
哟，　啊 夜 夜 的 晚　夕裏夢

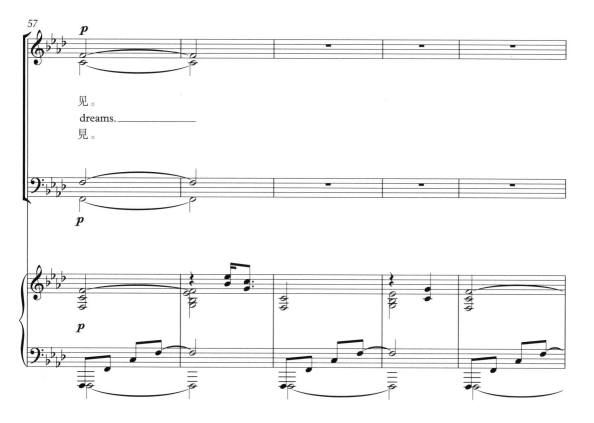

见。
dreams.
見。

3. 脚　踏　　　　上　大　路
3. Step - ping＿＿＿＿ on - ward,
3. 腳　踏　　　　上　大　路

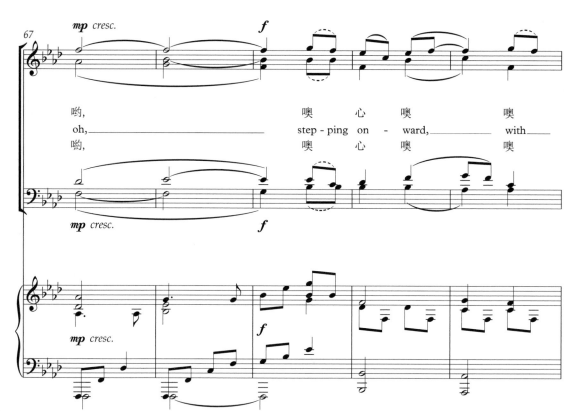

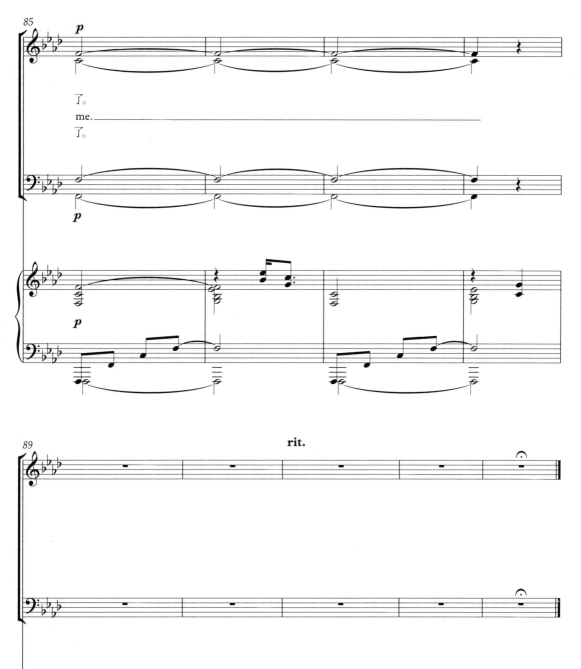

for David Hill and The Bach Choir

Mo Li Hua
(Jasmine Flower)
茉莉花

English words by Bob Chilcott

Trad. Chinese
arr. BOB CHILCOTT (b. 1955)

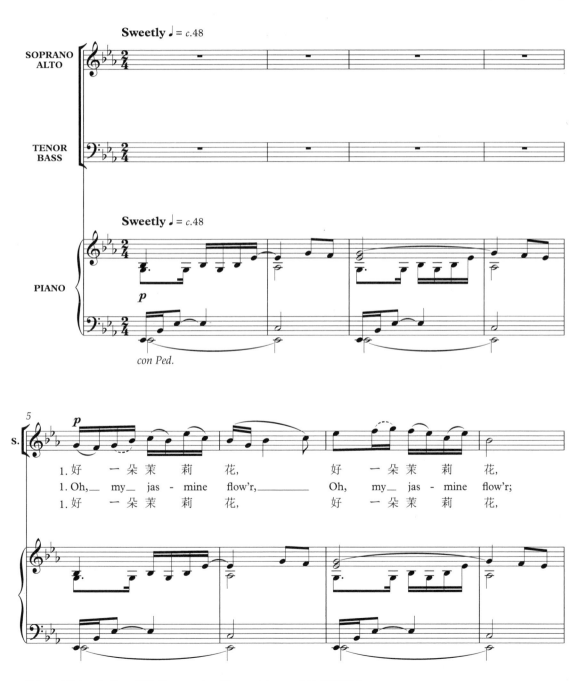

满园 花开 香也香 不过它，
Your sweet-est fra-grance lin-gers, lin-gers in the air;
滿園 花開 香也香 不過它，

我有心 采 一朵戴 又怕看花 的
If I were to pluck your blos-som, Ev'-ry-one would scold me for
我有心 採 一朵戴 又怕看花 的

人 儿 骂。
what I had done.
人 兒 罵。

mp
2.好 一朵
2.Oh, my
2.好 一朵

mp
2.好 一朵茉莉
2.Oh, my jas-mine
2.好 一朵茉莉

采 一 朵 戴 又 怕 来 年 不 发
pluck your blos-som You_ might ne - ver_ come a-gain a - no - ther____
採 一 朵 戴 又 怕 來 年 不 發

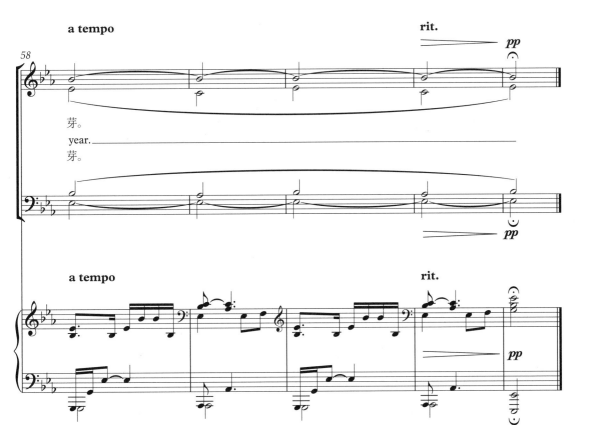

芽。
year._____
芽。